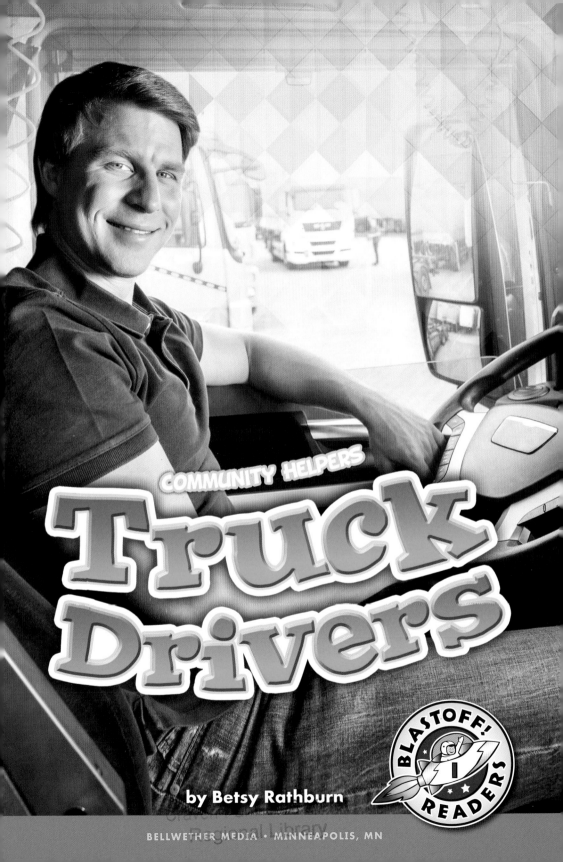

COMMUNITY HELPERS

Truck Drivers

by Betsy Rathburn

BELLWETHER MEDIA • MINNEAPOLIS, MN

BLASTOFF! READERS

Note to Librarians, Teachers, and Parents:

Blastoff! Readers are carefully developed by literacy experts and combine standards-based content with developmentally appropriate text.

Level 1 provides the most support through repetition of high-frequency words, light text, predictable sentence patterns, and strong visual support.

Level 2 offers early readers a bit more challenge through varied simple sentences, increased text load, and less repetition of high-frequency words.

Level 3 advances early-fluent readers toward fluency through increased text and concept load, less reliance on visuals, longer sentences, and more literary language.

Level 4 builds reading stamina by providing more text per page, increased use of punctuation, greater variation in sentence patterns, and increasingly challenging vocabulary.

Level 5 encourages children to move from "learning to read" to "reading to learn" by providing even more text, varied writing styles, and less familiar topics.

Whichever book is right for your reader, Blastoff! Readers are the perfect books to build confidence and encourage a love of reading that will last a lifetime!

This edition first published in 2020 by Bellwether Media, Inc.

No part of this publication may be reproduced in whole or in part without written permission of the publisher. For information regarding permission, write to Bellwether Media, Inc., Attention: Permissions Department, 6012 Blue Circle Drive, Minnetonka, MN 55343.

Library of Congress Cataloging-in-Publication Data

Names: Rathburn, Betsy, author.
Title: Truck Drivers / by Betsy Rathburn.
Other titles: Blastoff! readers. 1, Community Helpers.
Description: Minneapolis, MN : Bellwether Media, Inc., 2020. | Series: Blastoff! Readers: Community Helpers |
    Includes bibliographical references and index. | Audience: Ages 5-8 | Audience: Grades K-1 |
    Summary: "Developed by literacy experts for students in kindergarten through grade three, this book introduces
    truck drivers to young readers through leveled text and related photos"– Provided by publisher.
Identifiers: LCCN 2019024618 (print) | LCCN 2019024619 (ebook) | ISBN 9781644871096 (library binding) |
    ISBN 9781618917898 (paperback) | ISBN 9781618917737 (ebook)
Subjects: LCSH: Truck drivers–Juvenile literature. | Truck driving–Juvenile literature. | CYAC: Truck drivers. |
    Truck driving. | LCGFT: Instructional and educational works.
Classification: LCC HD8039.M795 R37 2020 (print) | LCC HD8039.M795 (ebook) | DDC 388.3/44–dc23
LC record available at https://lccn.loc.gov/2019024618
LC ebook record available at https://lccn.loc.gov/2019024619

Editor: Kate Moening   Designer: Brittany McIntosh

Printed in the United States of America, North Mankato, MN.

C. 1

Table of Contents

On the Road Again

The truck driver
backs up to a
loading dock.
Special **delivery**!

loading
dock

The truck is quickly unloaded. Time to get back on the road!

What Are Truck Drivers?

Truck drivers bring supplies to homes and businesses. They drive big **semis** or small trucks.

semi

Many truck drivers travel across the country. Others work near home.

What Do Truck Drivers Do?

Truck drivers stop at stores and **warehouses**. They pick up and drop off deliveries.

Truck drivers keep their loads safe. They tie down loads with ropes and chains.

These helpers make sure trucks are safe to drive. They track problems in a **logbook**.

Truck Driver Gear

sunglasses   radio   logbook   rope

logbook

17

What Makes a Good Truck Driver?

Truck drivers work long hours. They need a lot of **energy**.

Overload Permit

5

Truck drivers watch out for other cars. They stop when they are tired. Drive safe!

Truck Driver Skills

- ✓ safe drivers
- ✓ energetic
- ✓ timely
- ✓ careful

Glossary

delivery

something brought from one place to another

logbook

a report of a truck's safety and a truck driver's day

energy

the power to work or move

semis

large trucks that can carry a lot

loading dock

an area near the back of a building where deliveries are loaded and unloaded

warehouses

buildings used to store a lot of things

To Learn More

AT THE LIBRARY
Liebman, Dan. *I Want To Be A Truck Driver.*
Richmond Hill, Ont.: Firefly Books, 2018.

Manley, Erika S. *Truck Drivers.* Minneapolis, Minn.:
Jump!, 2018.

Pettiford, Rebecca. *Big Rigs.* Minneapolis, Minn.:
Bellwether Media, 2018.

ON THE WEB

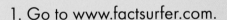

Factsurfer.com gives you
a safe, fun way to find
more information.

1. Go to www.factsurfer.com.

2. Enter "truck drivers" into the search box
   and click 🔍.

3. Select your book cover to see a list of related
   web sites.

Index